Ode to the City –
An Ethnographic Drama

Full details of all our other publications can be found on http://www.multilingual-matters.com, or by writing to Multilingual Matters, St Nicholas House, 31–34 High Street, Bristol, BS1 2AW, UK.

Ode to the City –
An Ethnographic Drama

Adrian Blackledge and Angela Creese

MULTILINGUAL MATTERS

Bristol • Jackson

DOI https://doi.org/10.21832/BLACKL5171
Library of Congress Cataloging in Publication Data
A catalog record for this book is available from the Library of Congress.
Names: Blackledge, Adrian, author. | Creese, Angela, author.
Title: Ode to the City – An Ethnographic Drama/Adrian Blackledge and Angela Creese.
Description: Bristol, UK: Jackson: Multilingual Matters, 2022. | Includes bibliographical references. |
    Summary: "This ethnographic drama script is adapted from observations conducted in a large city centre
    library in the UK. It is a creative curation of field notes, transcripts, audio recordings, video recordings,
    conversations, and observations. The ethnographic drama tells a story of political tension in everyday life
    at a time of austerity" – Provided by publisher.
Identifiers: LCCN 2021052851 (print) | LCCN 2021052852 (ebook) | ISBN 9781800415164 (paperback) | ISBN
    9781800415171 (hardback) | ISBN 9781800415188 (pdf) | ISBN 9781800415195 (epub)
Subjects: LCSH: Intercultural communication–England–Birmingham–Drama.
    | Multilingualism–England–Birmingham–Drama. |
    Librarians–Language–England–Birmingham–Drama. | Municipal
    government–England–Birmingham–Drama. | LCGFT: Drama.
Classification: LCC P94.65.E75 B53 2022 (print) | LCC P94.65.E75 (ebook) | DDC 303.48/20942496–dc23/
    eng/20211116
LC record available at https://lccn.loc.gov/2021052851
LC ebook record available at https://lccn.loc.gov/2021052852

British Library Cataloguing in Publication Data
A catalogue entry for this book is available from the British Library.

ISBN-13: 978-1-80041-517-1 (hbk)
ISBN-13: 978-1-80041-516-4 (pbk)

Multilingual Matters
UK: St Nicholas House, 31-34 High Street, Bristol, BS1 2AW, UK.
USA: Ingram, Jackson, TN, USA.

Website: www.multilingual-matters.com
Twitter: Multi_Ling_Mat
Facebook: https://www.facebook.com/multilingualmatters
Blog: www.channelviewpublications.wordpress.com

The policy of Multilingual Matters/Channel View Publications is to use papers that are natural,
renewable and recyclable products, made from wood grown in sustainable forests. In the manufac-
turing process of our books, and to further support our policy, preference is given to printers that
have FSC and PEFC Chain of Custody certification. The FSC and/or PEFC logos will appear on
those books where full certification has been granted to the printer concerned.

Typeset by R. J. Footring Ltd, Derby, UK.
Printed and bound in the UK by the CPI Books Group Ltd.

Contents

Acknowledgements

This work was supported by the Arts and Humanities Research Council (1 April 2014–March 2018) as a Translating Cultures Large Grant: 'Translation and Translanguaging. Investigating Linguistic and Cultural Transformations in Superdiverse Wards in Four UK Cities' (AH/L007096/1), Principal Investigator, Angela Creese. With Mike Baynham, Adrian Blackledge, Jessica Bradley, John Callaghan, Lisa Goodson, Ian Grosvenor, Amal Hallak, Jolana Hanusova, Rachel Hu, Daria Jankowicz-Pytel, Li Wei, Agnieszka Lyons, Bharat Malkani, Sarah Martin, Emilee Moore De Luca, Jenny Phillimore, Mike Robinson, Frances Rock, James Simpson, Caroline Tagg, Jaspreet Kaur Takhi, Janice Thompson, Kiran Trehan, Piotr Wegorowski and Zhu Hua. Further information about the research project is available at https://tlang.org.uk.

We are particularly grateful to Rachel Hu, who was a key member of the research team in the collection, transcription, translation and analysis of linguistic ethnographic material.

Preface

This script is adapted from ethnographic observations conducted in a large, new, city-centre library in the UK. In the research we asked how people communicate in public settings when they bring into contact different biographies, backgrounds and languages. When we came to select a site for research, we approached the state-of-the-art Library of Birmingham, the largest regional library in Europe. The library attracts a diverse constituency of users, including local people from the city, and visitors from all over the world.

One of the library staff agreed to be a key participant. She was originally from Hong Kong, having moved to the UK nearly 20 years earlier. Over four months we observed her working in the library. Our colleague Rachel Hu shadowed the key participant as she went about her daily routine. We (Adrian, Angela and Rachel) wrote field notes which described what we saw and heard as we observed. We gave the key participant a digital voice recorder, to record her spoken interactions with members of the public and colleagues. She also recorded during her tea breaks and lunch breaks.

When we first negotiated access to do the research, the library was a beacon of civic pride for the city. Record-breaking numbers of people had visited in the 12 months since it had opened. The spectacular building had exceeded every criterion for success. But by the time we started our field work, six months later, the government had made cuts to local authority grants. The city's finances were hit hard. Opening hours were significantly reduced, and the library announced that it would cut more than 50% of its staff.

The ethnographic drama script represents discourses in circulation at a moment of political tension. The action focuses on the staff room in the library, where the fictionalised characters of four customer experience assistants take their lunch and tea breaks. The ethnographic drama is not a verbatim account of research data. It is a creative curation of field notes, transcripts, audio-recordings, video-recordings, conversations and observations. It is both ethnographic fiction and creative non-fiction.

Setting and Characters

The staff room of a large, new, city-centre library. The year is 2015.

ABBI   A customer experience assistant in the Business and Entrepreneurship section of the library, in her twenties.

ANGEL   A customer experience assistant in all sections of the library, in her fifties.

JOE   A customer experience assistant in the Children's section of the library, in his thirties.

RAJ   A customer experience assistant in the Heritage and Archive section of the library, in her forties.

Act I

Scene 1

Angel, Abbi, Joe and Raj are on their break. They sit round a coffee-table.

RAJ   They said either you go for VR or you have to apply for your own job.

ANGEL   VR? What's VR?

ABBI   Voluntary redundancy.

JOE   They pay you off and that's it, you're finished.

ANGEL   Why would you apply for that?

JOE   If you don't, you could end up with nothing.

ABBI   Some of us will end up with nothing either way.

ANGEL   Why's that?

ABBI   If you've been working for the council for less than two years you don't qualify for redundancy pay.

ANGEL   So what's the point of going for VR then?

ABBI   Exactly.

ANGEL   Wait. You either apply for VR or end up with no job?

ABBI   Or you apply for your own job and you might still end up with nothing.

JOE   They've got you either way.

ABBI   But if you've been working here a while, you do get redundancy pay.

RAJ   A week's pay for every year.

ABBI   How long have you worked for the library service?

ANGEL   Me? Eighteen years.

JOE   So it would be your weekly wage times eighteen.

RAJ	Isn't it one and a half week's pay for each year after you were forty-one?
ANGEL	Forty-one?
RAJ	A few pounds more.
ABBI	Better than a slap in the face with a wet fish.
ANGEL	I don't know. Is it?
RAJ	What's the union doing about it?
ABBI	Apparently there's nothing they can do.
JOE	The money's run out.
RAJ	The money's run out? It's less than eighteen months since we had Malala.
ABBI	Malala Yousafzai.
RAJ	Malala Yousafzai opening the library, unveiling the plaque. What was it she said?
ANGEL	A room without books is like a body without a soul.
ABBI	That's it.
RAJ	A body without a soul, that's what this place is going to be.
ANGEL	We were all so proud, a beautiful building.
RAJ	The biggest library in Europe.
JOE	Award-winning design.
ABBI	What was the name of the government minister?
ANGEL	He gave a speech.
ABBI	I remember.
RAJ	He said the library was an ode to the city.
ABBI	A symbol of the future.
ANGEL	The future didn't last very long.
JOE	They're going to get rid of a hundred staff.
ANGEL	A hundred? There can't be more than two hundred people work here now.
ABBI	One hundred and eighty-three.

ANGEL   It's more than half.

ABBI   More than half.

ANGEL   And you have to apply for your own job?

RAJ   Or go for VR.

ANGEL   It's not exactly a choice, is it?

JOE   Library services used to be a job for life.

RAJ   Working for the council used to be a job for life.

JOE   We don't exactly do it for the money.

RAJ   It's serving the public, isn't it? Helping the public.

JOE   You do wonder if the city council has any idea what we do here.

ANGEL   People come for information.

ABBI   Get help to find a job.

RAJ   For that little bit of support.

JOE   Like with teaching their children to read.

ABBI   To apply for a course.

RAJ   Find out about their ancestors; do their family tree.

JOE   Read a book with their children. It makes all the difference.

RAJ   Some don't even know what they're looking for.

JOE   Before they know it, they've found something.

ANGEL   That bit of hope, that sense of direction.

ABBI   It isn't only the city council, though, is it? The government has stopped the grant, cut the grant to the council.

ANGEL   But, then again, you go back to why they have to do that. Go back to the financial crash, and you have to ask who was responsible, who was looking after the shop at that time.

JOE   Yeah, but....

ABBI   The most savage cuts to any council in the country. Ever.

ANGEL   Who was in charge of that mess? It happened on Labour's watch.

ABBI   It was a global crisis, though, a global recession. It wasn't our ... it wasn't the British government. It started in America.

JOE   Like the Spanish flu.

ANGEL   On Labour's shift, and you have to ask....

ABBI   You can't say.

RAJ   The other thing is, who was running the council when they decided
           to invest in a new library they obviously couldn't afford?

ABBI   I think people are willing to pay. They believe in the library. They'll
           pay a few more pounds on their council tax if it means they have
           one of the best libraries in the world.

RAJ   When they took that decision, the Tories were running the city.
           They left it in the lap of the Labour group.

ABBI   It's something for the city to be proud of. It's a beacon for the city,
           the jewel in the crown.

RAJ   Not anymore. It's something for the city to be ashamed of.

ABBI   I wouldn't say that.

ANGEL   A white elephant is what it is.

JOE   It doesn't help, though, does it? Blaming this lot or that lot.

RAJ   We can't just sit here and do nothing.

JOE   The fact is that a hundred people are going to lose their jobs. It
           could be any of us. It will be. A hundred people.

RAJ   We have to fight back. We have to fight the cuts. There's a rally on
           Saturday, isn't there?

ANGEL   For all the good it will do.

Scene 2

Angel, Abbi, Joe and Raj are on their break. They sit round a coffee-table.

ANGEL   Who's taking over as Director?

RAJ   They've brought someone in as interim.

ANGEL   Interim?

RAJ   She's supposed to be temporary.

JOE   A hit squad?

RAJ   What?

JOE   Someone to come in, sack half the staff, slash expenditure, run the place down, and leave with no strings.

ANGEL   And a fat wallet.

JOE   Someone with no investment in the place.

ANGEL   Or the people.

RAJ   Why did he go?

JOE   Did he jump?

RAJ   Or was he pushed?

ANGEL   Why would he stay? All the years of planning, all the promises, and at the last minute, when everything's finished, the building completed, the staff in post.

JOE   The high-profile opening ceremony.

ANGEL   They pull the rug out from under him.

RAJ   You couldn't make it up.

JOE   Do you know where he's gone?

ANGEL   The official line is that he's retired.

RAJ   Just like that?

ANGEL   Who knows? What we do know is that he's gone.

Joe	And they've brought this new person in.
Abbi	What will it mean for us?
Raj	It's not likely to be good.
Angel	You don't know.
Raj	We'll have to wait and see.
Joe	Did you see the line of people this morning?
Abbi	I know. All the way down to Symphony Hall.
Joe	There must have been a thousand people.
Angel	They didn't know about the change to opening times.
Abbi	They weren't happy.
Angel	Some of them had been queuing for two hours.
Joe	Queuing two hours to get into the library.
Raj	They were singing.
Joe	[*Sings*] Why are we waiting, why-y are we waiting, why are we waiting?
Abbi	A man tried to sneak in with me. Security had to stop him.
Joe	You shouldn't have to deal with that.
Raj	When you're going into work.
Angel	People don't expect it.
Raj	They're used to the library opening at nine o'clock.
Joe	You can't blame them for being upset.
Angel	All the doors were locked, but the café was open.
Raj	Anything to make money.
Abbi	It was cold.
Raj	Too cold to stand outside for two hours.
Joe	I would have gone home.
Angel	But if you've come on the bus....
Raj	An hour and a half journey.
Angel	You think you might as well wait.

Raj	Or you've wasted the whole day.
Joe	They can see through the windows; they can see inside the nice warm library.
Raj	They're used to going in.
Abbi	All the lights on.
Joe	The doors locked.
Angel	They started hammering on the glass.
Joe	Hammering.
Abbi	I thought they were going to break it.
Angel	Half a dozen people.
Joe	It's no fun for the security guards.
Angel	I was on reception.
Joe	I was talking to one of the security people.
Abbi	I could hear the hammering from the first floor.
Angel	Five or six people hammering with their fists on the glass.
Joe	He said the job has changed.
Angel	Kicking the glass.
Raj	Kicking?
Joe	He said it used to be about helping the public.
Angel	If they'd broken through….
Joe	Now it's crowd control.
Abbi	I could hear them kicking the glass. I could hear it from the first floor.
Joe	Dealing with complaints.
Angel	They were angry.
Joe	People are angry.
Angel	I don't frighten easily.
Raj	This is a library.
Abbi	It would be funny if it wasn't tragic.

RAJ   Funny?

ABBI   The citizens trying to smash their way into the library.

RAJ   Yes.

ABBI   So desperate to read a book.

RAJ   To educate themselves.

ABBI   To improve their minds.

RAJ   To better themselves.

ABBI   To discover new worlds.

RAJ   To find new stories, new adventures.

ABBI   Like a revolution.

RAJ   A revolution.

ABBI   So desperate.

RAJ   So desperate that they smash….

ABBI   Security stops them. They take matters into their own hands.

RAJ   Smash their way into the library.

ANGEL   It would be….

JOE   It would be funny.

ABBI   If it wasn't tragic.

ANGEL   Security called the police.

JOE   I didn't see them.

RAJ   Did they come?

ANGEL   I don't think they came.

Scene 3

Angel, Abbi, Joe and Raj are on their break. They sit round a coffee-table.

RAJ   I didn't see any of you at the rally on Saturday.

ANGEL   I was going to go, but it was so cold.

JOE   It was my day with the kids.

ABBI   You should have brought them.

RAJ   It was cold though.

ANGEL   I put my head out the door.

RAJ   The wind went right through you.

ABBI   I was there.

RAJ   Oh, I didn't see you.

ABBI   I arrived late. Jenny was going to come, but she decided to stay in bed.

RAJ   You're right, it was freezing, absolutely perishing.

ABBI   It's a shame. More people would have come.

RAJ   I thought there would be more people.

ANGEL   What was it like, then? A waste of time?

RAJ   Not at all; it was all right. It always makes a difference. You go out, it makes a difference.

ABBI   There were people giving speeches. You couldn't hear them very well because of the wind.

RAJ   Getting out and being seen, you know.

ABBI   That woman from Friends of the Library, she was good.

RAJ   Yes, I thought she was good.

ABBI   Very straightforward.

RAJ   And Women Against the Cuts.

9

ABBI   I didn't know the council is planning even bigger cuts for next year.

RAJ   There will be nothing left of this place.

ABBI   Death by a thousand cuts, she said.

RAJ   It is, though, isn't it?

ABBI   That was the other thing: she said there's a complete embargo on new acquisitions now. The public are being asked to donate their own books to the library.

RAJ   It would be nice to hear it first hand.

JOE   You might as well run a jumble sale.

ABBI   That's what it's going to be, a bring-and-buy sale, swapping each others' dog-eared Mills and Boons.

JOE   There was someone representing the Friends of Heritage and Archive.

ANGEL   How come Heritage and Archive has friends?

ABBI   It's a good question.

JOE   We don't have that in Children's.

RAJ   Everyone's a friend of the Children's section.

JOE   Was there a speaker from the union?

RAJ   There was, yes. She did all right. She had a go at the government, said they were hypocrites, which is right, but she seemed more set on defending the city council than anything else.

ANGEL   The union won't do anything.

ABBI   It's the government really, though, isn't it? I mean, there's no money for anything.

RAJ   And what's-her-name from the city council was there, the cabinet minister. Is that what they call her, the cabinet minister? She gave a speech. She looked really cold.

ANGEL   At least she turned up. At least she stood in front of the people and had something to say.

ABBI   She said the decision to reduce the library's staff and facilities is the most difficult decision the city council has ever had to make.

JOE   But is it a decision they have to make?

RAJ   She said it's all very well campaigning against the cuts to the library, but you have to make a choice between maintaining the library budget and protecting children's services.

ABBI   It's a false choice, though, isn't it? The council should be standing up against the cuts, not doing the dirty work of the Tories, saying you can cut this or cut that. It's a false choice.

RAJ   She said, can you look a child in the face and tell them you're not going to protect them anymore?

ANGEL   It's moral blackmail. If the government has made funding cuts, that isn't the fault of the tax payer, and it isn't the fault of the library staff.

RAJ   It isn't the fault of the children.

ABBI   They want you to make a choice and, of course, you're never going to choose to cut children's services, no one is.

ANGEL   So they make you choose cuts to the library.

ABBI   When all the time it's a false choice.

JOE   Not that anyone is saying it's easy for the council.

ANGEL   They have to balance the books in the end.

RAJ   That's what the cabinet minister said.

ABBI   It's a legal requirement.

ANGEL   They have to balance the budget.

ABBI   Then there was the poet, the what-do-you-call-it poet.

RAJ   Poet Laureate.

ABBI   Poet Laureate. He did a poem in support of the library.

JOE   Yes?

RAJ   It wasn't the best poem in the world.

ABBI   It wasn't Billy Bragg.

RAJ   They should have asked Billy Bragg.

ABBI   Then the speeches ended.

RAJ   And we all marched down New Street.

ABBI   As far as the Bullring.

RAJ   Not everyone did.

ABBI   It was really cold by then.

JOE   It was on *Midlands Today*, Satnam Rana.

ABBI   Was she there?

RAJ   Were we on? I didn't see.

JOE   They had the cabinet minister, and they had the poet.

RAJ   We stood around for a bit. We didn't really know what to do. We got colder and colder.

ABBI   Some of us went to Costa.

RAJ   Some of us left.

ABBI   There were police everywhere at the station. I think Blues must have been at home.

Scene 4

Angel, Abbi, Joe and Raj are on their break. They sit round a coffee-table.

ANGEL	Did you see *Silent Witness*?
ABBI	I was out last night.
ANGEL	So clever, the way they....
JOE	What I can't understand is why there always has to be a murder in the first five minutes of every episode.
ANGEL	It's a crime drama.
JOE	No explanation, no motivation, nothing.
ANGEL	It all works itself out.
ABBI	We went to the new curry place.
ANGEL	There's always a reason in the end.
JOE	A reason?
ANGEL	The deaf mute girl, then the teacher.
RAJ	The fifth murder was different.
JOE	It's gratuitous though, isn't it?
ANGEL	There's going to be a reason for everything.
ABBI	I didn't see it, but....
ANGEL	It carries on next week. It's all going to make sense in the end.
RAJ	Then the sniper phones the police inspector.
ANGEL	I'm unstoppable, he says, unstoppable.
RAJ	Unstoppable.
ANGEL	Unstoppable.
JOE	What I don't like is, not only that show, but every time you turn on the television, always a young woman being murdered.

RAJ   That's what it is though.

JOE   Always really gruesome.

RAJ   It's a crime drama.

JOE   It's just standard now, a young woman murdered in terrifying circumstances, psychopathic killer on the loose, police fumbling about, sudden breakthrough, scary final scene, killer apprehended or shot dead.

RAJ   Not always the same.

JOE   Life isn't like that: there isn't a crazed murderer on every corner.

ANGEL   You don't have to watch it. There are other channels.

JOE   It's the same though, it's the same. Every drama on every channel, the same story. There's nothing original.

RAJ   It's the longest-running crime drama. Millions of people watch it. All those people can't be wrong.

JOE   Can't they?

ANGEL   They must be doing something right.

JOE   It's not really an argument, is it? A lot of things are popular. It doesn't make them any good. *Coronation Street.*

ABBI   *EastEnders.*

JOE   *Hollyoaks.*

RAJ   Soaps are soaps though.

ANGEL   People like them.

JOE   Exactly.

RAJ   It's about taste.

JOE   You don't want a taste for violence.

ABBI   A taste for murder.

JOE   Some things are better quality than other things, that's all.

ANGEL   That's different.

RAJ   It's entertainment.

JOE   I'm sorry, I don't find murder entertaining.

ANGEL   But you know it isn't real.

Raj	It's only a story.
Abbi	But it's….
Angel	All made up.
Raj	Only a story.
Joe	It's just….
Angel	All pretend.
Joe	Not what I call entertainment.
Raj	You can switch off though, can't you?
Joe	I know I can.
Raj	If you don't like it.
Joe	Obviously.
Raj	Switch off and read one of your books.
Joe	Obviously.
Raj	I'm just saying no one makes you watch it.
Angel	No one makes anyone watch it.
Joe	I'm not.
Raj	Make a cup of tea. Wait for the news to come on.
Joe	It's not about me.
Raj	By the time you've made yourself a cup of tea….
Angel	Had a Garibaldi biscuit….
Joe	I don't need you to tell me.
Raj	The news will come on.
Joe	I'm only saying.
Raj	You can watch real people blowing each other to bits.
Angel	On the news.
Joe	I'm not arguing about that.
Abbi	There's no need.
Angel	What are you arguing about?
Joe	I'm not even arguing.

RAJ   It sounds like you're arguing.

JOE   I'm trying to say, all I'm trying to say….

ABBI   It's not worth falling out, is it?

RAJ   Turn it over to the other side.

ANGEL   Switch it off.

RAJ   Make a cup of tea.

ANGEL   Let people watch what they want to watch.

ABBI   I don't think he's saying….

RAJ   Live and let live.

JOE   I'm not saying, I would never say….

ANGEL   That's it, live and let live.

          [*Pause*]

ABBI   We went to the new curry place on Stratford Road, the one that used to be a bingo hall. It was a church before that. The waiters wore turbans and frock coats.

          [*Pause*]

          We were the only people there. I had the vegetarian thali. Jenny had lamb bhuna. And a garlic naan. She wasn't that impressed. Overpriced, too.

Scene 5

Angel, Abbi, Joe and Raj are on their break. They sit round a coffee-table.

ANGEL   Don't forget to vote, don't forget to vote.

ABBI   I already voted on the way to work.

ANGEL   Who did you vote for?

ABBI   You're not supposed to tell, are you?

ANGEL   Why?

ABBI   It's a secret ballot.

ANGEL   Yes, but….

ABBI   It's private.

ANGEL   It's only us.

ABBI   My dad always says you never tell, it's secret.

JOE   Is it the first time you've voted?

ABBI   First time in a general election.

JOE   You don't have to say.

ABBI   First time to vote in the government.

RAJ   Don't tell. You're right.

JOE   It's no one's business.

ABBI   I don't mind saying, it's….

RAJ   No, don't say, don't say.

ABBI   I voted Labour. There, I said it.

RAJ   Good for you.

ANGEL   Ed Miliband, I can't get on with him, his voice.

ABBI   My family always votes Labour.

JOE   It's true, he doesn't come across well in the media.

RAJ	His policies are all right.
ANGEL	Did you see that picture of him with the bacon sandwich?
JOE	You want someone to look prime ministerial.
RAJ	It's when he speaks.
ABBI	It's about the policies though, isn't it?
JOE	No, you're right.
ABBI	You can't vote against him because someone put a bacon sandwich in his hand and started snapping away with a camera.
JOE	No.
ANGEL	Cameron has already said this will be his last time.
RAJ	Then who will we have?
ABBI	He'll hand over to Osborne.
RAJ	Like Blair and Brown.
JOE	Watch out for Boris.
ANGEL	He's done a good job as Mayor of London.
JOE	Has he?
ABBI	They won't allow him to be leader. Will they?
RAJ	You don't know. He plays the clown, but I've heard he's ruthless underneath.
ANGEL	You might need that. A good leader has to be tough.
RAJ	Is he standing in the election?
JOE	Uxbridge and South Ruislip.
ABBI	Safe seat.
RAJ	I didn't know he was even standing again.
ABBI	If you vote Tory you'll get a referendum.
ANGEL	Referendum?
JOE	On Europe.
ABBI	Cameron promised it.
JOE	They made him promise.

ABBI	Backed him into a corner.
JOE	Backed himself into a corner.
RAJ	Come on, there's no way people would support leaving Europe.
ABBI	You've got UKIP pushing for it.
ANGEL	Farage is popular. People like him.
ABBI	That's why voting Labour's the only way.
ANGEL	I mean, I don't....
RAJ	I can't see it. Leaving Europe would be crazy.
JOE	People want change.
ANGEL	They've had enough of austerity.
RAJ	What's that got to do with the EU?
ABBI	What was it Tony Blair said? It's like in *Blazing Saddles*.
RAJ	I love *Blazing Saddles*.
ABBI	The scene where the sheriff holds a gun to his own head, and says 'Do what I want or I'll blow my brains out'.
ANGEL	Who's the sheriff though?
ABBI	If we vote for Cameron again we might end up blowing our own brains out.
RAJ	It's never going to happen. We're part of the European Union. One of the longest-established members. You can't just leave.
JOE	You're right.
RAJ	It would be crazy.
JOE	It would be. Crazy.
RAJ	You're not voting Conservative are you?
ANGEL	I might, I might. You never know. We'll see when I go into the polling booth. We'll see.
RAJ	You're joking, aren't you?
ANGEL	No. I haven't made up my mind.
RAJ	You're going to vote for the same government that has cut the budget so we all have to apply for our jobs, or take redundancy. We don't want them in again, do we?

ANGEL   What are the options? Miliband, Clegg, Farage. I don't know. We'll see. We'll see.

JOE   You have to look beyond the personalities though.

ABBI   When I finish work I'm going on the knock.

RAJ   Good for you.

ABBI   There's a group of us. We'll go together.

ANGEL   You do what?

ABBI   Knock people's doors, check that they've voted. Make sure all the votes come in.

RAJ   Is Jenny going?

ABBI   She is, yeah. She'll do the driving.

RAJ   Driving who?

ABBI   Anyone who can't get to the polling station. Anything we can do to get the vote out.

ANGEL   What have people been saying on the doorstep?

ABBI   It's mixed. A lot of don't knows, a few don't cares.

ANGEL   Not everyone even votes.

JOE   You have to vote. It should be compulsory.

ABBI   A lot of people want Cameron out but they can't see an alternative.

ANGEL   They're all the same in the end.

ABBI   I wouldn't say that.

ANGEL   Politicians.

ABBI   I wouldn't say they're all the same.

RAJ   We can't have four more years of this.

JOE   Five, it will be.

RAJ   Five more years of this.

ABBI   What you have to worry about is if they win a clear majority.

JOE   That's it.

ABBI   The coalition has been bad enough.

RAJ   It's a strange thing. Days like this. It's democracy. You have the election.

JOE	You're waiting.
RAJ	You put your cross on the paper.
ABBI	Post it in the ballot box.
JOE	And you're waiting.
ANGEL	Will you stay up all night?
ABBI	I will.
JOE	I'll stay up. I won't sleep anyway. I might as well stay up.
RAJ	I can't stay awake all night. I'll watch the exit poll. I might watch until midnight. That's it for me.
ANGEL	It won't change the result.
RAJ	That's right. It won't change the result.
ANGEL	You might as well go to bed.
RAJ	With your fingers crossed.

Act II
Scene 1

Angel, Abbi, Joe and Raj are on their break. They sit round a coffee-table.

ANGEL   What's that?

RAJ   Last night's leftovers. Nothing exciting.

ANGEL   Leftovers? Looks nice.

RAJ   I put it in the microwave.

JOE   Smells good.

RAJ   Beef stroganoff. My husband cooked it.

ANGEL   What's in it?

RAJ   Beef, mushroom, mustard, thin sauce. I don't know.

ANGEL   Thin sauce?

JOE   Stroganoff. Hungarian?

RAJ   My husband said Bulgarian. Could be Hungarian.

ABBI   Stroganoff? Isn't that Russian?

RAJ   Stroganoff? Not Russian. Is it?

JOE   No, Hungarian. Is it Russian?

RAJ   I don't think so.

ANGEL   Don't look at me.

JOE   I would have said Hungarian.

ABBI   Here you are. [*Reads from her phone.*] Wikipedia. A Russian dish of sautéed pieces of beef served in a sauce with smetana.

RAJ   Smetana?

ABBI   Sour cream.

Joe	You live and learn.
Abbi	Named after noble Count Stroganoff.
Angel	You did say Russian.
Raj	They were talking on the radio this morning about Russian interference in the election.
Joe	Russian interference?
Abbi	Who was?
Raj	That Labour MP, the Welsh one.
Abbi	Which?
Raj	He was involved in the phone hacking thing, years ago.
Angel	Labour would say that, wouldn't they, now they've lost.
Abbi	What was he saying about Russia?
Raj	About cyber attacks.
Joe	Cyber attacks?
Abbi	In the general election?
Angel	How do they?
Joe	Who in Russia?
Abbi	What is a cyber attack anyway?
Raj	They didn't really say.
Angel	Is it when a computer attacks another computer?
Abbi	What's that got to do with the election?
Joe	Through your email.
Angel	You lose all your data.
Joe	Open an attachment that has a virus.
Angel	Millions of messages at the same time.
Joe	If you don't recognise it, don't open it.
Angel	We had that training day.
Joe	They get into your systems.
Angel	Start to take control.

JOE	Explore your networks.
ANGEL	Make changes.
JOE	Install their own scanning tools.
ANGEL	For their own benefit.
JOE	Disrupt normal business.
ANGEL	Overload the internet.
JOE	Delete the whole operating system.
ABBI	But the election?
RAJ	You can see how it happens.
ABBI	Does it affect how you vote?
JOE	They change things on Facebook.
RAJ	Twitter.
JOE	You don't know.
ABBI	Isn't it just conspiracy theory?
RAJ	That's it, they don't know.
ABBI	Who?
JOE	We don't know.
RAJ	Next time we have to guard against it.
ABBI	Next time?
RAJ	The next election.
ANGEL	Who knows who the candidates will be then.
RAJ	Miliband's resigned.
JOE	And Clegg.
ANGEL	And Farage.
JOE	It's going to be last man standing.
RAJ	Labour needs a woman leader.
ANGEL	Who?
RAJ	The one married to Jack Dromey, what's her name?
ANGEL	Who?

RAJ   Labour woman.

JOE   I know who you mean.

RAJ   She was on a lot during the election.

JOE   Or the one married to Ed Balls.

ABBI   He lost his seat.

RAJ   You mean Yvette.

JOE   Cooper, that's it, Yvette Cooper. She's good.

ANGEL   She's not very tall.

ABBI   We need someone who will put a more radical agenda to the people.

JOE   But who?

ABBI   I agree we need a woman, but Yvette Cooper and Harriet Harman are both too close to Miliband.

RAJ   Harriet Harman, that's who I was thinking of.

JOE   There will be a leadership election.

ABBI   We need a more radical voice, a radical agenda.

RAJ   That's it, Harriet Harman.

ABBI   I'm so tired.

RAJ   Did you stay up all night?

ABBI   Until four o'clock.

JOE   At least Farage didn't get in.

ABBI   I couldn't stand it anymore, so depressing.

RAJ   The Greens did all right.

ABBI   It's not much of a consolation.

JOE   The SNP did well.

ABBI   Labour got wiped out in Scotland.

JOE   Completely.

ABBI   Fifty seats.

JOE   Fifty-six out of fifty-nine.

RAJ   A landslide.

ABBI   Unbelievable.

ANGEL   Was it the Russians?

RAJ   Who knows? You know....

ANGEL   Who knows?

Scene 2

Angel, Abbi, Joe and Raj are on their break. They sit round a coffee-table.

ANGEL   You're young.

RAJ   You'll find something else.

ANGEL   It'll be the end for me.

ABBI   There's nothing out there.

ANGEL   At my age.

ABBI   Young people are suffering.

ANGEL   What can I do?

ABBI   There's nothing.

JOE   Make yourself indispensable.

ANGEL   Oh yeah.

JOE   Aren't you doing the Chinese book collection?

ANGEL   I'm not.

JOE   No?

ANGEL   I used to be, but since the move....

JOE   Tell them.

ANGEL   I do it voluntary.

JOE   Tell them they need you.

ANGEL   Not really my job.

JOE   Tell them you're the only....

ANGEL   I am, but....

JOE   Tell them there's no one else.

ANGEL   I don't know.

JOE   No one else speaks Cantonese. No one can read the books.

ANGEL   No, but….

JOE   That's your hook.

ANGEL   I….

JOE   That's your niche.

ANGEL   Used to be.

JOE   Your USP.

ANGEL   USP?

JOE   Tell them.

ANGEL   I will.

JOE   You will?

ANGEL   I will tell them.

JOE   Tell them.

ABBI   There's nothing out there.

RAJ   Have you looked?

ABBI   This is a good job.

RAJ   It was a good job.

ABBI   I don't want to give it up.

RAJ   It's going to be different.

JOE   No services.

RAJ   No activities.

JOE   Nothing for the community.

RAJ   No human contact.

ANGEL   It's all going to be run by machines.

RAJ   Self-service.

ABBI   If you hang on….

RAJ   It won't be the same.

ANGEL   Nothing public facing.

RAJ   It's going to be a warehouse for old books.

ABBI   They say the library will come back in the future.

JOE	Come back?
ABBI	Revive. The building, come back better than ever. They can't just….
JOE	It won't.
ABBI	If they just keep it going.
RAJ	Five more years.
ABBI	Find a way, just hang on.
JOE	Five more years.
ABBI	When things are better.
JOE	Who will?
RAJ	It's too late.
ABBI	You have to hope.
RAJ	Hope doesn't feed hungry families.
ABBI	You have to.
RAJ	We don't know that things will get better.
ABBI	You….
JOE	The government won't.
ANGEL	Or the council.
RAJ	They don't believe in culture.
ABBI	If….
RAJ	They don't believe in community.
ABBI	If you….
RAJ	They don't believe in public service.
ABBI	If you don't….
RAJ	Apply for your job.
JOE	You're right.
RAJ	You're young.
JOE	You have to hope.
ABBI	You have to hold on.
RAJ	Apply for your job and see what….

JOE	Things have been bad before.
RAJ	See what happens.
JOE	Apply for your job.
RAJ	See what happens.
JOE	See what happens.

Scene 3

Angel, Abbi, Joe and Raj are on their break. They sit round a coffee-table.

ABBI	I was in the reading area today.
JOE	The readers' section?
ABBI	Where the newspapers and magazines are.
JOE	The readers' section.
ABBI	Where the orange sofas are.
JOE	Okay.
ABBI	By the coffee machine.
JOE	Yes.
ABBI	There was a man.
JOE	A man in the readers' section.
ABBI	Not on the sofa.
JOE	Okay.
ABBI	In one of the armchairs.
JOE	Yes.
ABBI	He might have been homeless.
JOE	Very likely.
ABBI	The smell.
JOE	People come in.
ABBI	I never smelled anything like that.
JOE	Come in off the street.
ABBI	I looked at him.
JOE	Yes.
ABBI	His mouth open.

JOE	Okay.
ABBI	Saliva dribbling down his chin.
JOE	Mm hm.
ABBI	I went a bit closer.
JOE	Went a bit closer to….
ABBI	He was lying.
JOE	Lying.
ABBI	On his back in the chair.
JOE	Yes.
ABBI	Legs apart.
JOE	Mm.
ABBI	I went closer.
JOE	Yes.
ABBI	To look.
JOE	Yes.
ABBI	I couldn't see whether….
JOE	Whether?
ABBI	He was breathing.
JOE	Oh.
ABBI	His lips looked blue.
JOE	Really?
ANGEL	Was he?
ABBI	The slightest bit blue.
JOE	Okay.
ABBI	I put my face to his face.
JOE	I see.
ABBI	The smell.
JOE	Yes.
ABBI	It made me feel ill.

Joe	The smell.
Abbi	I still couldn't tell.
Joe	No.
Abbi	Whether he was breathing.
Joe	No.
Raj	Was he?
Abbi	His lips the slightest bit blue.
Joe	Yes.
Abbi	There was this notebook.
Joe	Notebook.
Abbi	The pages covered in tiny writing, blue ink, careful, tiny writing on the pages of this notebook.
Joe	Writing.
Abbi	Every page of this notebook.
Joe	The writing.
Abbi	The notebook was small.
Joe	Yes.
Abbi	Every page, tiny writing, blue ink.
Joe	You had a look.
Abbi	Some of it was in red ink.
Joe	Yes.
Abbi	Some of it written top to bottom.
Joe	Oh.
Abbi	Not side to side.
Joe	Mm.
Abbi	Like a great writer fallen on hard times.
Joe	Could be.
Abbi	I placed the notebook in the pocket of his, of his….
Joe	Yes.

ABBI   Of his cardigan, red cardigan, under his....

JOE   His....

ABBI   Under his coat.

JOE   Coat.

ABBI   Cardigan seen better days.

JOE   Oh.

ABBI   Great writer.

JOE   Hard times.

ABBI   Sleeping in the library.

JOE   People do.

ABBI   Nowhere to go.

JOE   No.

ABBI   Only the library....

JOE   That's it.

ABBI   When I placed the notebook....

JOE   Yes.

ABBI   He made this noise.

JOE   Oh.

ABBI   Like a horse.

JOE   A horse?

ABBI   A sort of snort.

JOE   A horse?

ABBI   The noise a horse will make when it's irritated by a fly.

JOE   A horse.

ABBI   To clear its nostrils.

JOE   Yes.

ABBI   I thought he was going to wake up.

JOE   Yes.

ABBI   He didn't wake up.

JOE	No.
ABBI	He was alive.
JOE	Yes.
ABBI	Sleeping.
JOE	Yes.
ABBI	A great writer, fallen on hard times, sleeping in the library.

Scene 4

Angel, Abbi, Joe and Raj are on their break. They sit round a coffee-table.

ANGEL   Why did the city council spend one hundred and eighty-eight million pounds on a new library at the same time as we were hit by a global recession?

RAJ   They say the decision was taken before the credit crunch.

ANGEL   That doesn't mean they can't change their minds.

ABBI   Why did they go ahead?

ANGEL   Hubris.

ABBI   Who?

ANGEL   Hubris. They wanted the biggest and best public building in Europe.

RAJ   In the world.

ANGEL   Yes, in the world.

RAJ   And having announced they would build it, they didn't have the guts to change their minds.

ANGEL   No.

RAJ   They wanted a symbol, a beacon, something that said this is who we are: proud, confident, affluent, a twenty-first-century city.

ABBI   It is a beacon. It does say those things.

JOE   And people like it. They are proud of the library.

ABBI   The biggest library in Europe.

JOE   It's a spectacular building.

ABBI   And it's more than a building.

JOE   Award-winning architecture.

ANGEL   But in eighteen months it's gone from being a beacon of success to an embarrassment.

RAJ   And you have a Labour council, come on, a Labour council about to issue redundancy notices to one hundred of its own staff.

ANGEL   It's unbelievable.

ABBI   But isn't the government to blame, rather than the council?

RAJ   The government's slashed council funding, so yes, that's part of the problem.

ANGEL   But the council could have pulled out as soon as they knew the library was going to be a financial burden.

JOE   It was used to paper over the cracks of the council's problems.

RAJ   It was head-in-the-sand time.

ANGEL   Storing up trouble, pretending this day would never come.

RAJ   They needed to sort out the money first.

ANGEL   Never anything for community libraries away from the city centre.

RAJ   Where people actually live, in the neighbourhoods where they really need a library.

ANGEL   It was like, look at us, we have this beautiful, impressive new building, that's who we are, but all the time....

RAJ   And we already had a library in the city centre.

ANGEL   I liked the Central Library.

ABBI   Was that the one Prince Charles said...?

RAJ   Looked like a place where books are incinerated, not kept.

ANGEL   He made it famous.

ABBI   I was watching yesterday. They were demolishing it.

RAJ   A lot of memories in there.

ABBI   They spray water constantly.

ANGEL   The dust.

ABBI   Risk of fire.

RAJ   It was special.

ABBI   A lot of people say that.

RAJ   I studied there for my degree.

ABBI	They are taking it apart piece by piece.
RAJ	I would be there for hours and hours.
ABBI	As if they want to rebuild it somewhere else.
JOE	Like London Bridge.
ANGEL	The Reference section was huge.
RAJ	It was a serious place.
ANGEL	Not so much the lending.
RAJ	And the music library. You could borrow anything you'd ever heard of. Go home with LPs. You didn't have to buy them. There was more trust.
ABBI	LPs?
ANGEL	You had to show them your stylus.
JOE	Stylus? What is…?
ANGEL	Your cartridge.
JOE	I don't….
ANGEL	For your record player. In those days.
JOE	Your needle?
ANGEL	Your needle, from your record player, your stereo.
ABBI	They pull down a wall and you can see right inside.
RAJ	A lot of history.
ANGEL	People's lives.
RAJ	It was there less than forty years, so not ancient history, but personal history, forty years out of a life.
JOE	People talk about it. They miss it.
RAJ	Always calm, quiet, studious, you could guarantee.
ANGEL	The largest non-national library in Europe at that time.
RAJ	I didn't know.
ANGEL	Apparently.
RAJ	A space where I could study and learn, without responsibility for anything or anyone. No pressure other than the pressure I put on myself.

ABBI	I'll think of you when I'm watching the demolition tomorrow.
RAJ	You might see my ghost.
ABBI	When the wall comes down.
RAJ	I'll be there. On the fourth floor.
ABBI	I'll look for you.
RAJ	Sitting over my books, notepad and biro, reading, taking notes.
ABBI	When the wall comes down.
RAJ	I won't even notice the demolition.
ABBI	Nose to the grindstone.
RAJ	Glance up, see the wrecking ball, the excavator, the library open to the elements.
ABBI	Straight away return to your books.
RAJ	Straight away return to my books.
ABBI	My mum used to bring us when we were kids.
RAJ	She did?
ABBI	Every month.
RAJ	That's nice.
ABBI	The Children's section was really good.
RAJ	Yes.
ABBI	We spent hours in there. *Not Now Bernard*, *Where the Wild Things Are*, *Willy the Wimp*. I loved those books.
RAJ	You might see yourself as a ghost, too.
ABBI	I might.
RAJ	A ghost child, reading.
ABBI	I love this library. But it's true, the memories are all in the old one.
RAJ	I was talking to someone yesterday who said he was part of the original construction team for the Central Library.
JOE	In the seventies?
RAJ	Early seventies. He was quite emotional. It means something.
ANGEL	This place is going to be like a ghost town soon.

ABBI   The *Marie Celeste*.

JOE   If everyone loved the old library so much, why did they knock it down?

ANGEL   Probably the Prince Charles effect.

RAJ   Good old Charlie. Thanks a lot.

ANGEL   He could have minded his own business.

ABBI   It's progress, isn't it? You have to move forward.

ANGEL   Progress.

RAJ   One step forward, two steps back.

ANGEL   Onward, forward.

RAJ   Take the second on the right for the dole queue.

ANGEL   Do they still call it the dole queue?

RAJ   Quick, march.

Act III
Scene 1

Angel, Abbi, Joe and Raj are on their break. They sit round a coffee-table.

JOE	Did you put in for it?
ANGEL	I put in for both.
ABBI	Both?
RAJ	I thought you couldn't.
ANGEL	What have I got to lose?
ABBI	True.
RAJ	I didn't.
JOE	You didn't?
RAJ	I'm not going to fill in any more of their forms.
JOE	But....
RAJ	If they don't know the kind of job I do by now, they haven't been paying attention.
ANGEL	Good for you, good for you.
JOE	It's all been put on hold anyway.
ABBI	What has?
JOE	The VR. The job interviews.
ABBI	Why has it?
ANGEL	Something to do with the union negotiating with the city council.
JOE	You don't know whether you're coming or going.
ANGEL	Apply for VR. Don't apply for VR. Apply for your job. Don't apply for your job. It's chaos.

JOE   In the meantime, what are we supposed to do? Look for something else? Sit tight until they make up their minds?

RAJ   They don't care. We're expendable. They'll get rid of more than half of us one way or another. But I'm not going to beg.

JOE   That might be what they want. That might be part of a deliberate strategy. Create uncertainty, put doubt in our minds, and we start to leave of our own accord, start to drift away.

RAJ   I'm not playing their games, that's all.

ANGEL   I'd like to go part time.

ABBI   You would?

ANGEL   I've always wanted to study.

ABBI   What, for a degree?

ANGEL   English literature. I love reading. *Middlemarch*. *Jane Eyre*. Shakespeare.

RAJ   You should definitely do it.

ANGEL   It's my dream.

ABBI   Turn it into an opportunity.

RAJ   Go for it.

ANGEL   If I can reduce my hours, and work part time.

JOE   Have they offered that?

ANGEL   No.

RAJ   I don't think so.

ABBI   You can always ask.

ANGEL   Yes.

JOE   I haven't applied for my job either.

RAJ   Really?

JOE   Something might be telling me to move on.

RAJ   Yes?

JOE   It might be time to go.

ANGEL   You don't know.

JOE	I'd rather make a positive decision myself than hang around hoping to be one of the chosen few.
ABBI	You're right. It's divisive. Everyone looking over their shoulder, watching each other, thinking will it be me or her, will they keep their job, will I be the one to go.
JOE	When I came to this country I found a roof over my head, but I needed work. This came up. It was supposed to be six months' maternity cover, and here I am three years later.
ABBI	They kept you on?
JOE	Extended my contract. Eventually they had to make me permanent. Which turns out to be a bit of a joke now.
ANGEL	Permanent. Yeah.
JOE	So I will go.
RAJ	What will you do?
JOE	I have something in the pipeline. Community arts. If that doesn't come off, we'll see.
ABBI	I'm worried it will be a case of last in, first out.
RAJ	Do you want to stay?
ABBI	I like it on the business desk. You really feel you can make a difference, help people. They appreciate you.
RAJ	I don't know whether it will be the same. There will be changes. It won't be the same job.
ANGEL	We won't be able to provide the same support to the public. It's all going to be self-service.
RAJ	All done by computers. Sometimes you need that human contact.
ANGEL	You have to have the conversation.
ABBI	I'll stay if they let me. I don't want to give up this job.
ANGEL	Are you going to the union meeting, then?
ABBI	It's not only union. It's management as well.
JOE	Friday morning, isn't it?
RAJ	Before opening.
ABBI	We have to come in early.

RAJ   Nine thirty.

ANGEL   I wouldn't expect too much.

RAJ   Whatever they say they'll change their minds two minutes later.

JOE   Let's see what they have to say first.

ABBI   Maybe they've found a way to stop the cuts.

ANGEL   Maybe the council has won the lottery.

RAJ   The rollover prize!

JOE   One hundred million!

ABBI   And we can all keep our jobs!

Scene 2

Angel, Abbi, Joe and Raj are on their break. They sit round a coffee-table.

RAJ   I'm trying to give up coffee. But you get to this point in the afternoon.

ANGEL   Nothing else will do.

RAJ   You need that kick to wake you up.

ANGEL   Wake you up, yeah.

RAJ   It's not so bad now the opening hours are shorter.

ANGEL   That last hour used to be hard.

JOE   I stopped drinking coffee.

ANGEL   You did?

JOE   Two months ago. I used to be on ten or twelve cups a day.

RAJ   That's a change then.

ANGEL   Do you feel better for it?

JOE   I can't say that I feel any different, quite honestly.

RAJ   You do wonder.

ANGEL   Whether it's as bad for you as they say.

RAJ   What do you drink instead of coffee then?

JOE   I've really got into tea. There's a whole thing.

RAJ   I like nice tea.

JOE   There's a place in the Bullring.

RAJ   I know it.

JOE   Jasmine Pearls. That's a green tea.

RAJ   Have you tried Silver Needle?

JOE   And Oolong tea.

ABBI   Tea's definitely better for you than coffee.

JOE	Better than twelve cups a day.
RAJ	Everything's bad for you these days though, isn't it?
ANGEL	Butter.
RAJ	Yes.
ANGEL	One minute they say only eat spread made from vegetable oil made with saturated fats.
RAJ	Saturated or unsaturated?
ANGEL	Could be unsaturated.
RAJ	Yeah.
ANGEL	Whatever you do, never touch butter.
RAJ	It's the work of the devil.
ANGEL	Especially salted butter.
RAJ	Dairy fat.
ANGEL	Then the next minute they say the opposite.
RAJ	The opposite.
ANGEL	Butter is good for you.
RAJ	Eat as much as you like.
ANGEL	Don't bother with low-fat spread.
RAJ	Trowel on the butter.
ANGEL	Trowel on the butter.
RAJ	You don't know which way to go.
ANGEL	You don't know what to believe.
RAJ	You don't.
ANGEL	The same with eggs.
RAJ	Eggs?
ANGEL	Exactly the same. Eggs are bad for you.
RAJ	Eggs aren't bad for you.
ANGEL	Eggs.
RAJ	I never heard that. Eggs.

ANGEL	Bad for your heart.
RAJ	Come on.
ANGEL	Go to work on an egg.
JOE	Now red wine.
ANGEL	That's another one.
JOE	One glass a day is good for you.
ANGEL	One glass?
JOE	Then, before you know it, one glass a day is bad for you.
RAJ	Why?
JOE	Cancer, heart, liver, kidneys.
RAJ	One glass of wine?
JOE	Red wine.
RAJ	That's me finished then.
JOE	You don't know.
RAJ	You don't know what to believe.
ABBI	My dad says a little of what you fancy.
JOE	Does you good.
ANGEL	Exactly.
JOE	Your dad knows his onions.
ABBI	Literally. And his garlic.
RAJ	Garlic?
ABBI	On his allotment.
ANGEL	Garlic?
ABBI	Hard neck, soft neck.
RAJ	What is?
ABBI	From the Isle of Wight.
ANGEL	Hard neck?
RAJ	This is garlic?
ABBI	Elephant garlic.

ANGEL	Elephant?
ABBI	Huge.
RAJ	Elephant?
ABBI	Black garlic.
ANGEL	No.
ABBI	Like liquorice.
RAJ	The garlic is?
ABBI	More proud of his black garlic than anything.
RAJ	On his allotment?
ABBI	Sits there for hours watching it grow.
RAJ	Not much to see.
ABBI	Checking for rust.
RAJ	Rust?
ANGEL	Not rust.
ABBI	White rot. Yellow spot. Thrips.
RAJ	What's thrips?
ABBI	More proud of his black garlic than anything. Literally.

Scene 3

Angel, Abbi, Joe and Raj are on their break. They sit round a coffee-table.

ANGEL   I'm none the wiser.

RAJ   It was a talking shop.

JOE   They go round in circles.

ABBI   Back to square one.

ANGEL   So what they're saying now is the union....

ABBI   The union won concessions.

RAJ   Concessions.

JOE   Concessions that mean there will be no compulsory redundancies.

ABBI   Unless the number of voluntary redundancies is insufficient to stabilise the financial situation.

RAJ   Which means?

ABBI   We're still in the same position.

JOE   We're still in the same position we were in before the meeting.

ABBI   What was she saying about applying for re-employment?

RAJ   About applying for your own job?

ANGEL   When you apply for your own job....

JOE   There are new criteria.

RAJ   If you don't meet the criteria.

ABBI   You've been doing your job all this time, doing a decent job, no one ever said anything about....

ANGEL   No, it's new. You have to meet....

JOE   You have to meet the new criteria.

ABBI   I've already applied.

RAJ	You can leave your application in.
JOE	Or start again.
ABBI	I didn't know about the new criteria.
RAJ	They only said it today.
ABBI	I didn't know.
JOE	Nobody knew.
ABBI	I didn't know.
ANGEL	Nobody knew.
RAJ	What will you do?
ANGEL	I'm going to apply.
JOE	Apply again?
ANGEL	Apply again.
ABBI	It's so long.
RAJ	A test of patience.
JOE	Endurance.
RAJ	You stay in the game.
ABBI	She said she wants to treat everyone fairly.
JOE	Or you walk away.
ABBI	She said she wants everyone....
RAJ	Play the game by their rules.
JOE	Or don't play at all.
ABBI	She said she wants to....
ANGEL	I'm going to.
ABBI	Wants to give everyone an equal....
RAJ	On their terms.
ABBI	Equal opportunity.
JOE	They move the goalposts.
ABBI	To meet....
RAJ	You hit your target.

JOE	They change the target.
ABBI	To meet the criteria.
ANGEL	I'm going to apply again.
RAJ	Nothing is enough.
ABBI	Meet the criteria.
RAJ	You achieve your goal.
ABBI	The new criteria.
JOE	They move the goalposts.
ABBI	The union said....
RAJ	Complex negotiations.
ABBI	The union....
ANGEL	Across the table.
RAJ	Wrestling with the detail.
ANGEL	Burning the midnight oil.
RAJ	Irresistible force.
ANGEL	Immovable object.
RAJ	Impasse in the talks.
ANGEL	Head to head.
ABBI	Rumours of progress.
RAJ	Hint of a breakthrough.
ABBI	The smallest concession.
RAJ	Finally a deal.
JOE	Hard-won compromise.
ANGEL	Mutual agreement.
RAJ	Balanced and reciprocal.
ANGEL	No compulsory redundancies.
JOE	No compulsory redundancies.
RAJ	Unless there are not enough.
JOE	Unless there are not enough voluntary....

RAJ	Not enough voluntary redundancies.
ANGEL	No compulsory redundancies.
JOE	Unless there are.
RAJ	Unless there are.
ABBI	That's the same.
JOE	It's the same.
ANGEL	The same.
RAJ	The only people who have to go.
JOE	Are the people who don't want to go.
ABBI	That's the same.
ANGEL	Apply for VR.
RAJ	Or apply for your job.
ANGEL	Or both.
RAJ	No guarantees.
ABBI	That's the same.
JOE	It's the same.

Scene 4

Angel, Abbi, Joe and Raj are on their break. They sit round a coffee-table.

ANGEL   We used to be always laughing at coffee-time.

RAJ   That's true.

JOE   We still have a laugh.

ANGEL   Not like we used to.

RAJ   Does anyone know any jokes?

ANGEL   I don't mean like actual jokes.

JOE   What?

ANGEL   Everything's more serious. Everything is.

ABBI   It's the waiting.

ANGEL   It makes you anxious.

JOE   What?

ANGEL   It makes you tense.

ABBI   All we're doing is waiting for someone else to make a decision about our future. We have no control over anything.

RAJ   Knock knock.

ANGEL   Who's there?

RAJ   Jeremy.

ANGEL   Jeremy who?

JOE   Man walks into a bar.

ABBI   We wait.

JOE   Orders a drink.

ABBI   You don't know how long.

JOE   Sits down next to a horse.

ABBI   No information.

JOE   Looks at the horse.

ABBI   Nothing.

JOE   Says….

RAJ   Why the long face?

JOE   Why the long face?

ABBI   Waiting.

JOE   Horse walks into a bar.

ANGEL   I heard a joke the other day.

JOE   Go on then.

ABBI   You can't make plans.

ANGEL   Two men decide the way to make their fortune….

ABBI   Jenny talks about buying a house.

RAJ   That's nice.

ANGEL   Is to buy a greyhound.

ABBI   We can't even go to the bank.

ANGEL   So they buy this greyhound.

RAJ   Have you got your eye on something?

ABBI   We can't even talk to the bank.

ANGEL   They buy this greyhound.

RAJ   Do you know which area?

ANGEL   From a man in the pub.

ABBI   We can't even go and discuss a mortgage.

JOE   Of course.

ANGEL   And put it in a race.

RAJ   How many bedrooms?

ABBI   You need a letter from your employer before they'll even talk to you.

ANGEL   It comes last.

ABBI   You can't get a letter from your employer if you're under threat of a
          redundancy notice.

JOE   No.

ANGEL   The following week they put it in another race.

RAJ   Have you looked at anything?

ANGEL   In the second race it comes last.

ABBI   I would ask my dad to lend us the deposit.

JOE   Will he?

ANGEL   They decide the greyhound needs more training.

RAJ   What does Jenny do again?

ANGEL   They train it every evening for two hours.

ABBI   I might not be able to pay him back.

RAJ   If you lose your job.

ABBI   If I lose my job.

ANGEL   The more the dog trains the more it eats.

JOE   It's difficult.

ANGEL   The more it eats the more expensive it is.

ABBI   Like your life is on hold.

RAJ   Yes.

ANGEL   They put it in a third race.

ABBI   You're waiting.

ANGEL   For a third time it comes last.

RAJ   Frustrating.

JOE   Annoying.

ABBI   You can't make any decisions.

ANGEL   First man says to the second man….

RAJ   No.

JOE   What does Jenny say?

ANGEL   We have to get rid of the greyhound.

ABBI   She's the most patient person in the world.

ANGEL   Second man says, how?

Abbi	But….
Joe	It can't be easy.
Raj	It's a shame.
Angel	First man says we could tie a brick to it and chuck it in the cut.
Abbi	I mean, it's all right, we're all right as we are.
Raj	But you want to buy.
Abbi	Jenny wants….
Angel	Second man says we can't chuck the dog in the cut.
Abbi	Jenny wants to buy a house.
Joe	And you?
Angel	First man says, what then?
Raj	Second man says, we can sell it.
Joe	What does your dad say?
Angel	First man says, we can't sell it, no one will buy that dog.
Abbi	I haven't….
Raj	He doesn't…?
Angel	Second man says, what then?
Joe	You haven't?
Abbi	I….
Angel	First man says, I know what we can do.
Abbi	I don't want him to worry.
Raj	No.
Joe	No.
Angel	We can run and leave it.
	[*Pause*]
Joe	That's it?
Raj	I'm not sure why that's funny.
Joe	Because it's a greyhound?
Angel	It isn't real life.

ABBI   It's....
ANGEL   It's a joke.

Scene 5

Angel, Abbi, Joe and Raj are on their break. They sit round a coffee-table.

ANGEL   Debbie from the second floor said she's got a job at John Lewis.

JOE   Lucky her.

RAJ   Which department?

ANGEL   Customer support.

JOE   That's nice. Public facing.

ABBI   Not so different.

ANGEL   Less money, but more secure.

RAJ   You wouldn't have said that once.

ABBI   Will she get a discount?

ANGEL   That's what I said.

ABBI   What did she say?

ANGEL   After two months she gets twenty per cent.

RAJ   Twenty per cent?

ABBI   That's not bad.

RAJ   We should get to know her better.

JOE   I was talking to Pat.

ANGEL   Big Pat or Little Pat?

JOE   Little Pat.

ANGEL   Is she going?

JOE   She's applied for a hundred and sixty-seven jobs and only heard back from three.

ANGEL   She got interviews then?

JOE   Two rejections, one interview.

ANGEL   Where?

JOE   Working with children. She did say.

ANGEL   That's interesting work though.

RAJ   When is the interview?

JOE   This week, I think.

RAJ   I used to work with children, before I came here.

ANGEL   That's right.

RAJ   The children were lovely.

ANGEL   Hard work.

RAJ   Exactly. Every day you go home shattered. I'm not joking. It takes over your life. Really.

ABBI   Jenny says I should work with children.

JOE   Are you interested?

ABBI   She says I'm a natural. She says I should think about school teaching.

RAJ   Primary or secondary?

ABBI   She didn't say.

ANGEL   I don't think I would like to teach the very little ones.

JOE   I don't know. Teach them to read and write and all that. It could be quite rewarding.

RAJ   It's the little ones that wear you out.

JOE   My sister's a school teacher back home.

ANGEL   I didn't know you had a sister.

JOE   She teaches the older kids. Chemistry.

RAJ   Does she?

JOE   She's got a science degree.

ANGEL   You have to know what you're talking about.

RAJ   Are you going to apply for teacher training then?

ABBI   I don't know. I'll see what happens. I want to stay here if I can. I don't know whether I fancy teaching really.

ANGEL   One door closes and another one opens.

RAJ   Turn it into an opportunity.

ABBI   I'll see what happens.

RAJ   What's your subject?

ABBI   My degree was social anthropology.

RAJ   Oh, that's....

JOE   I know, it's....

ANGEL   What is?

ABBI   The study of societies and cultures.

JOE   Do schools?

ABBI   Schools don't.

JOE   As a subject.

ANGEL   History you could.

RAJ   Geography you....

ABBI   It's not....

JOE   Sociology you might.

RAJ   What do you actually...?

ABBI   Sort of what makes people tick.

ANGEL   Makes people?

ABBI   What makes them....

RAJ   Tick?

ABBI   Behave the way they do.

ANGEL   But you don't think....

ABBI   Jenny.

RAJ   You're not....

ABBI   I'm....

JOE   Secondary then, or...?

ABBI   I'm not....

ANGEL   Not in a rush to.

ABBI   I'll see what happens.

RAJ   You know Duncan in Archives?

ABBI   Duncan?

RAJ   In Archives.

ANGEL   The one with the beard.

RAJ   With the ginger beard.

ANGEL   Ginger.

RAJ   Tall.

ANGEL   Glasses.

ABBI   I don't.

RAJ   He used to be a teacher.

ANGEL   You should talk to him.

ABBI   What did he…?

ANGEL   Maths.

RAJ   Religious education. Wasn't it?

ANGEL   One of those.

ABBI   He was…?

RAJ   Secondary.

ABBI   What happened?

ANGEL   He didn't like it.

RAJ   Hated it.

ABBI   What was?

ANGEL   The pressure to get results.

RAJ   Results, results, results.

ANGEL   Sometimes you can't do it.

RAJ   The grades, the expectations, 'A's and 'A-stars'.

ANGEL   Nothing else would do.

RAJ   In the end, it's not about learning.

ANGEL   Not about the students.

RAJ   Not about knowledge.

ANGEL   It's all about results, all about league tables.

RAJ   He said schools are exam factories.

ANGEL   You do what you can to get everyone through. You give them help.

RAJ   You give them that extra bit of help.

ANGEL   You find a way to get them through.

RAJ   You find a way.

ANGEL   But it's never enough.

RAJ   Whatever you do.

ANGEL   He said it's constant pressure.

RAJ   Constant pressure.

ANGEL   He said, however hard you work....

RAJ   You ask yourself, is it worth it?

ANGEL   You wonder why you do it.

RAJ   Will you?

ABBI   I don't....

ANGEL   You won't?

RAJ   But it's good to have an ology.

ANGEL   An ology is always good.

RAJ   Social?

Act IV
Scene 1

Angel, Abbi, Joe and Raj are on their break. They sit round a coffee-table.

JOE	What did they ask you?
RAJ	Who was on the panel?
ABBI	Which office did you have to go to?
RAJ	Was it on the seventh floor?
JOE	How do you think it went?
ABBI	When will they let you know?
JOE	Did they ask you why you want to stay?
ABBI	Did they mention going part time?
RAJ	Is it the same job?
ABBI	Is it permanent?
JOE	Is it the same money?
RAJ	Is it still in customer experience?
JOE	When would it start?
ABBI	Did you have to do a presentation?
JOE	Is it the same hours?
RAJ	Did they ask about the union?
ANGEL	The union?
RAJ	Was there anything you couldn't answer?
JOE	How long did it last?
RAJ	How many questions were there?
JOE	Did they ask about VR?

RAJ   Did they know you've applied?

JOE   Did you tell them you're indispensable?

ABBI   Did you talk about your skills?

JOE   Did they ask about your languages?

RAJ   Did they ask about your experience?

JOE   Did they ask about the future?

ABBI   Did they ask about your plans?

RAJ   Did they ask if you're going to leave?

ABBI   Did they ask about your children?

RAJ   Did they ask about your husband?

ANGEL   I....

RAJ   Did you give a good account of yourself?

ANGEL   I don't....

ABBI   Did you do yourself justice?

ANGEL   I....

JOE   Did you tell them why they need you?

ANGEL   Not....

ABBI   Did you tell them what they would miss?

ANGEL   I....

RAJ   Did you tell them?

ANGEL   It's been so long since I....

JOE   You told them?

ANGEL   I didn't.

ABBI   What was the worst question?

ANGEL   I don't....

JOE   Was there anything you couldn't answer?

ANGEL   Not....

RAJ   There you are then.

ABBI   Did you ask them anything?

Joe	Did they let you?
Angel	I couldn't....
Raj	You answered all the questions?
Angel	I think....
Raj	Did they ask about income generation?
Angel	In...?
Abbi	Did they ask about corporate partnership?
Angel	Not....
Raj	Did they ask about flexible working?
Angel	I....
Joe	Was there anything they didn't ask you?
Angel	I'm not....
Raj	Did they give you scenarios?
Abbi	Scenarios?
Raj	Did they?
Angel	Not as....
Joe	Did you have to role play?
Raj	Did they put you in character?
Joe	Did you have to act it out?
Angel	I....
Raj	That's hard when they do that.
Joe	A difficult customer.
Raj	You're on reception.
Joe	Abusive.
Raj	Drunk.
Joe	You have to deal with them.
Raj	Act it out.
Joe	What you would say.
Abbi	Why?

RAJ   Like a test.

JOE   If you can handle it.

ABBI   In the interview?

RAJ   They can.

ABBI   Did they?

ANGEL   Not....

ABBI   Will they?

RAJ   They might.

JOE   Best to be ready.

ABBI   I don't....

ANGEL   They....

RAJ   How do you feel now?

JOE   How do you feel?

ABBI   How do you feel?

ANGEL   After eighteen years in the library they don't know me. As if all this time I've been invisible. It's like starting from scratch. Eighteen years of dealing with the public. Whoever comes to the desk, you listen, you engage, you find common ground. They can't speak English too well, but you find something in common. You go from there. Something. They speak Spanish, you try that out. They speak French, you give it a try. You find that common ground. People with no confidence, no self-esteem, don't know what to do with themselves, want to get on. People think nothing of themselves. People want a qualification. People want a job. People don't know what they want. People think they don't deserve anything. You pick them up. You point them in the right direction. You walk with them. You lead them by the hand. You help them navigate. You smile. You ask them. You listen. Sometimes they come because they're angry. They come because they need to be angry. You let them. You listen. You try to understand. You try. You don't always understand. You can't. You do your best. You always do your best. You're polite. You're courteous. You're convivial. You try. You make a difference. The slightest difference. Give people the help they need. They don't know. You try. You turn things round. They appreciate it. Day in, day out. Eighteen years. Thousands of people.

ABBI   But what?

ANGEL   You walk into an interview in the place you have worked for eighteen
        years, and they don't know you. You're invisible. They don't know
        what you've been doing all that time. They don't know the differ-
        ence you make. They don't know how you turn things around. You
        can't tell them. You try. You can't. They would have to be there. You
        can't tell them. They don't know. So you say nothing. You answer
        their questions. You say nothing.

Scene 2

Angel, Abbi, Joe and Raj are on their break. They sit round a coffee-table.

RAJ   So what's this new job, you said community arts?

JOE   Oh yeah. Nothing's settled yet, but....

RAJ   Where?

JOE   You know the old custard factory?

RAJ   No.

ABBI   I know, Deritend.

JOE   Near there. Digbeth.

ABBI   I know where you are, the new arts centre, you get the fifty bus.

JOE   That's it.

ANGEL   Community arts?

ABBI   On the creative side?

JOE   The job is more front of house, but I'd like....

RAJ   Get your foot in the door, that's it, work your way in.

JOE   That's what I thought, get a start.

ABBI   You'd like to...?

JOE   When I was at college, back home, I loved the theatre.

ANGEL   Treading the boards?

JOE   The smell of the greasepaint, as they say, all of that.

RAJ   My son was in a show.

ABBI   Really?

ANGEL   My niece went to drama school.

RAJ   He had to dress up as a girl.

JOE   I was in a play once.

ANGEL	Not RADA. What's the other one?
RAJ	My husband was mortified.
JOE	A friend of mine back home asked me to do it.
ANGEL	She's going to be in a West End show.
ABBI	I would have liked to go to drama school.
ANGEL	Something *Boots*.
JOE	I had to be on stage in a sack.
RAJ	*Boots*?
ABBI	My dad said it was too expensive.
JOE	I had to get out of the sack.
ANGEL	*Kinky. Kinky Boots, Kinky Boots.*
ABBI	*Kinky Boots*?
RAJ	That's what it's called?
JOE	Carry a second sack across the stage.
ANGEL	They're rehearsing now.
ABBI	Is she a singer?
ANGEL	And dancer.
JOE	Get back in the first sack.
ABBI	That's so glamorous!
RAJ	In the West End?
ANGEL	Almeida. Or Adelphi.
RAJ	*Kinky Boots*?
ANGEL	Transferred from Broadway.
ABBI	Wow.
RAJ	I haven't heard of it.
ANGEL	It isn't what she really wants to do.
ABBI	What does she want to do?
ANGEL	More serious theatre.
ABBI	Like what, Chekhov, or...?

ANGEL   She likes the avant-garde.

RAJ   Avant-garde indeed!

ABBI   I'd be scared of forgetting my lines.

JOE   There weren't any lines.

ABBI   It's amazing the way they remember.

JOE   Get out of the sack.

ABBI   Like say you're playing Hamlet.

ANGEL   I love Shakespeare.

JOE   Carry the second sack across the stage.

ABBI   Apparently Hamlet has more than fifteen hundred lines.

ANGEL   It's true.

JOE   Get back in the first sack.

ABBI   Can you imagine?

RAJ   It's more front of house though?

ABBI   Fifteen hundred lines.

JOE   To start with.

ANGEL   Get your feet under the table.

RAJ   You never know.

ANGEL   We'll be looking for your name in lights.

RAJ   Let us know when you're in something.

ANGEL   We'll come and see you.

ABBI   I'll definitely come.

JOE   I'll save you all tickets.

Scene 3

Angel, Abbi, Joe and Raj are on their break. They sit round a coffee-table.

ANGEL   Have you had your interview?

RAJ   I have, yes.

JOE   You have?

ABBI   I thought you weren't going to apply.

RAJ   I didn't.

ABBI   You said you weren't going to.

RAJ   I didn't apply for my job, and I didn't apply for VR.

ABBI   That's what I thought.

RAJ   They pulled me in anyway.

ANGEL   They interviewed you?

RAJ   They interviewed me for a job I didn't apply for.

JOE   That's crazy. What did they ask you?

RAJ   They asked me why I'm not applying for my job.

ANGEL   Ha ha. That's mad.

ABBI   What did you say?

RAJ   I said I'm not applying for my job because it's already my job.

ANGEL   What did they say?

RAJ   They said if I want to keep my job I have to apply.

JOE   What did you say?

RAJ   I said I'm not applying for my job because it's already my job.

ABBI   What did they say?

RAJ   They said there's a process.

ANGEL   Did they?

ABBI	What did you say?
RAJ	I said no process will make me apply for my own job.
ANGEL	Ha ha.
ABBI	What did they say?
ANGEL	They said if I don't abide by the process it will be worse for me.
JOE	What then?
RAJ	I said it's not logical for me to apply for my own job.
ANGEL	They can't argue with that.
JOE	So?
RAJ	They said technically it isn't my job.
ABBI	Technically?
RAJ	They said technically I've been dismissed. They said that's why I have to apply for my job.
ANGEL	What did you say?
RAJ	I said they can't dismiss someone without telling them.
ABBI	You did?
JOE	What did they say?
RAJ	They said I was looking for trouble.
ABBI	You're joking.
ANGEL	They said that?
RAJ	They said, what about your family?
JOE	Your family?
ABBI	What did they mean by that?
RAJ	I don't know.
ABBI	Then what happened?
RAJ	They gave me an application form.
JOE	Why?
RAJ	They put the form on the table in front of me.
JOE	What did they say?

RAJ	They said, all you have to do is sign.
ABBI	The application form?
RAJ	All you have to do is sign and you keep your job.
ANGEL	Just like that?
RAJ	All you have to do is sign.
ANGEL	Sign the form?
RAJ	Sign the form.
ABBI	I thought they were trying to get rid of us.
JOE	Half of us.
ANGEL	So you signed?
RAJ	I said it wasn't right.
ANGEL	Did you sign?
RAJ	I said it wasn't fair.
JOE	What did they say?
RAJ	They said, sign the form and keep your job.
ANGEL	So you signed?
RAJ	They gave me a pen.
JOE	You have to look out for yourself.
ANGEL	Did you sign?
ABBI	Did you?

Scene 4

Angel, Abbi, Joe and Raj are on their break. They sit round a coffee-table.

JOE   I see they've announced the candidates for the Labour Party leadership.

RAJ   There's a new system isn't there?

ANGEL   What is?

RAJ   Labour. They've got a new system to choose their leader.

ANGEL   Why?

RAJ   There was some scandal, so they changed it to one member one vote.

ANGEL   I thought the unions chose the leader.

JOE   Not only the unions.

RAJ   Not anymore, not in the new system.

ABBI   It's gone to one member one vote.

ANGEL   So anyone can become a member of the party and vote in the leadership election?

RAJ   Apparently.

ABBI   My dad said *The Telegraph* is telling Tories to join Labour and vote for Corbyn because he'll be a disaster and they'll never win another general election.

JOE   He's got a lot of support from young people.

ANGEL   If he gets in as leader it could be the end for Labour.

RAJ   Why?

ABBI   A lot of young people are looking at the options and saying he's different, more radical, speaks up for equality and social justice.

RAJ   Why would Tories?

JOE   Sounds to me like they're frightened of something.

ABBI	That's what my dad said.
RAJ	Frightened?
ABBI	It's democratisation. More people having a voice.
JOE	More people demanding change.
ANGEL	But they had that opportunity in the election. People didn't want it. They rejected it.
JOE	It could be the first time for generations there's a real chance of change.
ANGEL	I don't think people want it. In the end, I think people want things to stay the same.
ABBI	There's a leadership debate on BBC2 tomorrow, so we can make up our own minds.
JOE	Tomorrow?
RAJ	It clashes with *Britain's Got Talent* though.
ANGEL	Oh yes, the final. It's the final.
JOE	Did you watch it last week?
ABBI	We don't watch it.
ANGEL	I liked the magician.
RAJ	And the choir. I thought they were really good.
ANGEL	They were good. They could sing, but the songs were a bit boring.
RAJ	I liked them, beautiful singers, Welsh.
ANGEL	The magician was clever.
RAJ	And the impressionist as well.
JOE	He was funny.
RAJ	The dancers were all right.
ANGEL	The old ones or the young ones?
JOE	The boy band, not the old ones – they were embarrassing.
RAJ	Did you see them?
JOE	Why would you even do that in public?
RAJ	Who voted for them?

ABBI   When's it on?

JOE   What about the final? Who are you going to vote for?

ANGEL   You have to wait and see who's the best on the night.

RAJ   That dog's quite clever.

ANGEL   What's his name, Matisse?

RAJ   Matisse.

JOE   Matisse.

ANGEL   He is clever, with those tricks.

JOE   Won the public vote in the semi-final.

ANGEL   People like him.

ABBI   A dog?

RAJ   He's very cute.

ABBI   What does he do?

JOE   Performs on a tightrope.

ANGEL   And takes on a part. Like, last week he pretended to be a toy dog.

ABBI   The dog did?

JOE   So clever to train the dog to do that.

RAJ   I heard there are two dogs.

ANGEL   There are two dogs?

RAJ   They look the same. You can't tell them apart.

ANGEL   How does that work?

RAJ   Apparently one of them does the tightrope, the other does the acting.

ANGEL   Are you sure?

RAJ   I don't know. That's what someone said.

JOE   They didn't say that on the programme.

RAJ   Someone said. I don't know.

JOE   They said it was one dog.

RAJ   We assumed.

JOE	They said, didn't they say?
RAJ	They look the same.
ABBI	It won the public vote?
ANGEL	The dog did.
JOE	In the semi-final.
RAJ	Or two dogs.
ANGEL	Won the public vote.
JOE	Now it's the final.
ANGEL	People like the dog.
RAJ	Dogs.

Scene 5

Angel, Abbi, Joe and Raj are on their break. They sit round a coffee-table.

RAJ   What does it say?

ABBI   I can't even speak.

RAJ   Is it…?

ABBI   I can't.

JOE   What does it say?

ABBI   I….

RAJ   Do you want me to read it?

ABBI   Mm.

RAJ   'It is with regret I must inform you that your application for the post of customer experience assistant does not meet the prescribed criteria.'

JOE   Oh no. What else?

RAJ   'I wish you every success in your future endeavours.'

JOE   What? That's it?

ANGEL   It's like you never worked here.

JOE   No acknowledgement of your employment.

ANGEL   As if you're a complete stranger.

ABBI   I can't….

ANGEL   Prescribed criteria.

RAJ   Future endeavours.

JOE   What about their responsibility to you?

ABBI   I can't….

ANGEL   Your mortgage.

ABBI	No.
RAJ	Every success.
JOE	I know.
ANGEL	What are you going to do?
ABBI	I can't....
JOE	There's teacher training.
ABBI	I don't....
JOE	Those that can, do; those that can't, teach.
RAJ	What?
JOE	My sister says it. A joke. Those that can.
RAJ	It's not for now though, is it?
ANGEL	What are you thinking?
ABBI	I'm not.
JOE	Is there no explanation?
RAJ	That was the whole email.
JOE	Don't they owe you something?
RAJ	Surely.
JOE	Don't they have to say why you weren't successful?
ABBI	I don't....
RAJ	It doesn't make much difference.
JOE	They have a duty of care.
RAJ	You could ask for feedback.
ABBI	I don't....
JOE	You should. Ask them for the reason.
RAJ	We know the reason.
JOE	Make them say it.
ABBI	I....
JOE	They take someone on, they employ someone, they have responsibilities to that person. That's all I'm saying.

RAJ	You aren't going to change it.
JOE	They have responsibilities.
ABBI	I don't….
JOE	Everyone is entitled to know.
RAJ	Did they say when you'll find out about your application?
ANGEL	I got my email today as well.
RAJ	You did?
JOE	What did it say?
RAJ	Read it out.
ANGEL	I haven't got my phone with me now.
JOE	But you….
ANGEL	I got my job.
JOE	That's great.
RAJ	Well done.
ABBI	Congratulations.
ANGEL	But….
RAJ	But?
ANGEL	They won't consider my request for part-time employment.
JOE	They won't?
RAJ	Why?
ANGEL	They didn't say.
RAJ	What did they say?
ANGEL	'We are not able to consider…'.
JOE	That's it?
ANGEL	More or less.
JOE	Still, you got the job.
RAJ	That's good.
ANGEL	But studying will have to wait.
JOE	Yeah.

ANGEL	I'm a bit disappointed.
RAJ	Oh.
ANGEL	I thought it might be an opportunity.
JOE	To study.
RAJ	Still, you….
ANGEL	Yes.
	[*Pause*]
ABBI	I'm going to do it.
RAJ	You?
ABBI	I'm going to do it.
JOE	To do?
ANGEL	Teaching?
ABBI	The library might not want me.
RAJ	Well, the….
ABBI	But teaching.
JOE	Go for it.
ABBI	I'll make myself a teacher.
ANGEL	Are you sure?
ABBI	I'll be a teacher.
RAJ	You will.
ABBI	Jenny says I'm a natural.
JOE	You are.
ABBI	She says I need to be braver.
JOE	I don't know.
ABBI	Today I got braver.
RAJ	You'll be a great teacher.
JOE	You definitely will.
ANGEL	You'll be an inspiration.
ABBI	I don't know about that.

JOE   You will. You'll show them.

ABBI   An ordinary teacher.

JOE   You will.

RAJ   You will.

ABBI   I don't know.

ANGEL   You will.

ABBI   I'm going to try.